Changed!

by David Mayorga

SHABAR PUBLICATIONS
www.shabarpublications.com

Most Shabar Publications products are available at special quantity discounts for bulk purchase for sales promotions, fund-raising and educational needs. For details, write Shabar Publications at mayorga1126@gmail.com.

Changed! by David Mayorga
Published by Shabar Publications
3833 N. Taylor Rd.
Palmhurst, Texas 78573
www.shabarpublications.com
www.masterbuildertx.com

This book or parts thereof may not be reproduced in any form, stored in a retrieval system, or transmitted in any form by any means - electronic, mechanical, photocopy, recording, or otherwise - without prior written permission of the publisher, except as provided by United States of America copyright law.

Unless otherwise noted, all Scripture quotations are from the New Kings James Version of the Bible. Copyright@1979, 1980, 1982 by Thomas Nelson, Inc., publishers. Used by permission.

Cover by David Mayorga. *[I would like for the reader to note that the bleeding heart on the front cover is used to describe several things: First the heart of my King as He gave His life for me; secondly, it represents my sinful heart as it was rent because of my sin against God, and lastly, the continual brokenness that follows those who follow His ways and hunger and thirst for His righteousness.]*

Edited by Emily Rose King

Copyright @ 2021 by David Mayorga
All rights reserved

ISBN 978-1-955433-01-3

Table of Contents

Foreword 4

Introduction 11

Chapter 1: Born from Above! 18

Chapter 2: There is Power in the
Blood of Jesus! 26

Chapter 3: The Forgiven Life 41

Chapter 4: The Crucified Life 49

Chapter 5: The Resurrected Life 58

Chapter 6: Branded for Jesus! 68

Chapter 7: Are You Making Yourself
Available? 76

Chapter 8: The Ministry of Brokenness! ... 86

Chapter 9: The Gift of Faith Unleashed! .. 95

Chapter 10: Megaton Power! 104

Chapter 11: Have Thine Own Way Lord! 115

Chapter 12: In Case of Floods! 124

Foreword

I can remember meeting brother David like it was yesterday. We were speaking at a Men's Conference in central Florida. Several months before the conference, I was sent a copy of his book entitled, The Few, and I devoured it. It confirmed so much truth, that the Holy Spirit began to reveal Himself to me— it stretched my faith big time!

It was on the last night of the conference when David spoke, that the power of God filled the place, and touched every man present. We were getting ready to leave and I was talking to him about the school of ministry that he started in Texas. I said to him, "I would love to come to your school and learn from you."

Then he turned and said something that at the time, I thought was crazy and impossible: He said, "Jeremiah it isn't for you to come to my

Foreword

school; you will start your own school of ministry and you will even write your own training materials!"

Well, here I am almost 5 years later, and this prophetic word that he spoke to me, is now coming to pass right in front of my eyes. Brother David is one of the most humble and authentic men of God that I have ever had the privilege of knowing. You would be wise to pay attention to what he has to say.

"For I am not ashamed of the gospel of Jesus Christ, for it is the power of God for salvation to everyone who believes." (Romans 1:16)

This Scripture is a favorite for millions of believers everywhere. It's on t-shirts, bumper stickers, and all-over social media, yet many fail to ever experience its power. It is the power of God that changes us— so that we may please Him!

Foreword

When I encountered Jesus, I was homeless and had been addicted to heroin for 18 years. I was a liar and a thief. I was full of envy, bitterness, and anger; I was a manipulator and a sex addict; and to top it all off, I was an enemy and hater of God.

I blamed Him for making me the way I was. Sure, I had heard the gospel hundreds of times. I was raised in a Christian home, I prayed the prayer, I raised my hand, and was always promptly assured of my salvation — but I never experienced the power of God that could change me.

Would you please read that last paragraph again? Do you see what my problem was? It wasn't the drugs, and it wasn't the lack of believing in God. You can't be angry with someone you don't believe exists.

My revelation from God that changed everything, was that "I," was the problem! One day I woke up and realized this, and it was then and there, that

Foreword

I cried out to God knowing that if He didn't intervene to change me, I was going to die, hopelessly addicted to drugs and alone. That's when it all happened, right there under that highway overpass, I encountered Jesus the Son of the living God, and my life has never been the same ever since. That was the day I died; that was the day I denied myself, picked up my cross, and began to follow Jesus.

It wasn't just that one day though. I had to intentionally choose every single day afterwards to do the same and put off my old ways and patterns of thinking. My feelings could no longer be trusted, and I had to allow the cross of Christ to destroy my self-centered nature, every single day. I had to renew my mind by coming into agreement with what Jesus taught. What Jesus said was always right, whether I thought so or not; His ways were better whether I could do what He commanded or not. It was in this place where I finally learned that I could not do what He had

Foreword

commanded, because only He could do these things through the power of His Spirit working through me.

I was filled with a new hunger for the things of God, and I had to allow truth to pierce the deepest and darkest places of my heart. I had to allow and cultivate the resurrected life of Jesus to grow within me.

The words of the apostle Paul were finally made alive to me, "I have been crucified with Christ. It is no longer I who live, but Christ who lives in me, and the life I now live in the flesh I live by faith in the Son of God, who loved me and gave himself for me."

I was born again, and now I knew it was all real. I knew it was real because everything in me began to change.

Are you experiencing this power working in your

Foreword

life? Maybe you have but now you feel stagnant, like the fire isn't burning as hot as it once was. Maybe you have not (experienced this power,) but you're looking for answers and/or searching for truth. Maybe you are experiencing the power of God right now, but have very little practical understanding of how to cultivate it?

Think about it: Of all the books you could be reading right now, why do you think you chose this one? I can tell you with complete confidence, that it was not just by chance, it was by divine design. You thought you chose this book, but the reality is, you were chosen to read this book.

As you read Brother David's revelation, you will begin to feel the Spirit of Christ calling out to you — I believe you already feel it!

I am telling you with complete confidence that there is more in Jesus Christ than you have ever

Foreword

imagined possible. Don't allow yourself to settle for a gospel without the power to change you.

Jesus died for everyone, so that those who receive His new life will no longer live for themselves; instead, they will live for Him, who died and was raised for them!

Grace to you all through Jesus Christ our Lord,

    - Apostle Jeremiah Swartz, *Kingdom Tribe*
    Stanwood, WA

Introduction

As I began to unfold this manuscript to you, a question seems to always be in the forefront of one's Christian experience. The question is, How saved are you? What does this mean? It means how true, deep, or real is your born-again experience?

I believe that your initial born-again experience is very telling or at least very revealing of how your Christian walk will be. If your experience is a strong one — an experience that is deep-rooted in your innermost being — chances are that you will have the right mindset to overcome opposition easier than a person who didn't have this same experience.

Too many have made a decision to follow Christ without an actual experience of being born-again. They repeated the prayers, they made the vows, but they never entered into the death and resurrection of Christ. They saw the cross of Christ, but they never got on it!

If a person who has made the pledge to follow Jesus, doesn't get washed in the blood of Jesus for the forgiveness of his or her sins, and they fail to get on the cross and die to all their carnal desires— such a person will struggle to enter into the abundant life that Jesus promised!

There are many so-called believers in the church today who say that they are saved but their works deny their allegiance. Why is this? The reason for this is because these people were never born-again of the Spirit of God. These people offered prayers that were disengaged from the Spirit of God— prayers that were made without faith!

What Does an Empty Christian Life Look Like?

People who have attained some form of religion but have not entered into the power of God are

Introduction

always lagging behind. They don't come to the church, for they don't see the need to be fed. Why is this? Because they have no appetite!

When a baby is born, the baby usually comes out crying due to hunger! When a person is born-again from above, by the Spirit of God, a good sign that he is alive is that he or she is hungry!

Another characteristic of someone who has experienced God, is that now no one needs to push them to go after God. They invest into the kingdom of God. They buy a Bible and they read it and live it! This happens without anyone telling them to do it.

Another key thing is this: Truly born-again people stop whining, complaining, and criticizing. They are too caught up in knowing God that they don't have time to keep up with the person next to them and their hang ups.

Introduction

Before I close this introduction, I also want to know that people whose experience with God is not real, have a tendency to always struggle with spiritual forces. They are caught up in demonic spirits, shadows, and who is bewitching them. They are so focused on chasing demons that they are leaving the devil alone!

One of the things that I have seen true born-again believers gain is an identity in God. They discover immediately who they are in God. They learn quickly how much authority God has granted them and they learn to use it. They are no longer being pushed around; they are no longer being tossed back and forth by anyone.

A true born-again believer can see their future and not be afraid of it. They know God, they know themselves, and they know exactly what they are supposed to do with their lives.

The Pearl of Great Price!

Introduction

"Again, the kingdom of heaven is like a merchant seeking beautiful pearls, who, when he had found one pearl of great price, went and sold all that he had and bought it." (Matthew 13:45, 46)

If your experience with God didn't cost you anything, it probably didn't do anything inside of you! You see the mystery of the kingdom of God is that when you find what is valuable, (in this case it would be Jesus Christ) it's going to cost you everything to acquire.

If you have not sold your whole life to obtain Christ, I have my doubts that you have the abundant life that Jesus speaks of in John 10:10. You might have an external religion; you might have become a member of a certain church, but you do not know King Jesus and the life He offers you.

Listen to the story above: A merchant seeking beautiful pearls found one pearl. So, what did

Introduction

he do to acquire it? He went and sold all that he had— then bought it! You won't have Christ until you sell what is dear to you! Unless you allow God to take your most precious possessions, I'm afraid that you will never experience the life of God!

To be able to experience the power of the world to come, one must surrender all their life to Christ. One must allow God's Spirit to move in and take over. The power of the world to come is not religion and it's certainly not a feeling. The power of the world to come is a lifestyle that is led by the Spirit of God.

To be able to walk in this dimension of continuous victory, one must allow the Holy Spirit to be the leader. Only He knows that way of God, for He is the mind of God. Once the Spirit of God comes in— He will lead accordingly. The Spirit does not come to conform to our lifestyle; He comes to bring our lives up to where Christ

Introduction

is! He will lead us into all truth and show us the heart and mind of God on a daily basis.

Here's one thing that is special: The Spirit of God, once He makes His home within us, will provide government. We will never be lonely orphans again, and we will never be confused again! God will keep us in perfect peace!

Chapter 1

Born from Above!

"There was a man of the Pharisees named Nicodemus, a ruler of the Jews. This man came to Jesus by night and said to Him, 'Rabbi, we know that You are a teacher come from God; for no one can do these signs that You do unless God is with him.' Jesus answered and said to him, 'Most assuredly, I say to you, unless one is born again, he cannot see the kingdom of God.'" (John 3:1-3)

I want to begin this chapter by saying that unless a person is born from above, it will not only be hard to walk the Christian walk, but it will be impossible to do it! The power you need to please God is found in the miracle of the new birth (being born from above, from the Spirit of God). Without this experience, living for Jesus will be a nightmare.

Chapter 1: Born from Above!

Knowing You Have Been Born-Again

Now, let us look in more detail at what it means to be born-again— what it truly means to be born from above, just as Jesus explained to Nicodemus in John 3.

Being born from above means that God's holy Spirit has come to dwell inside of you; He has come to make His home in you because you have repented of your sins and washed yourself in the blood of Jesus. Unless repentance before God has been made and a washing of your sins through the blood of Jesus has been attained, your life remains separated from a holy God.

If a person at any place or at any time repents and washes themselves in the precious blood of Christ and then proceeds to invite the Holy Spirit into their own hearts, as to make Jesus Christ Savior and Lord, this individual has entered into the realm of God, the kingdom of God.

Chapter 1: Born from Above!

The Power of a New Life

As soon as a person opens their heart to Christ and invites Him to come and live within, the life of God, the breath of God enters in! This is powerful! This life is the very life of God living in your and through you! This is amazing!

The very life of God can be experienced and felt; it can also in many occasions even be seen in people's countenance. Where there used to be sadness, now there is joy. Where there used to be bondage, now there is freedom, and where there used to be guilt and shame, now there is confidence.

This is what the new life begins to do in the human vessel, as the Spirit of God comes to live within.

There is No Need for Anyone to Tell You!

Chapter 1: Born from Above!

Along with some of the common changes, we also find a convicting power. Things that we used to do are no longer at the top of our priority list. We no longer feel the need to do certain things to gain favor, please anyone or do them for selfish pleasure. Things are different now.

Interesting enough, the things we used to love, we now hate— the things we used to hate, we now love! This is all possible by the new birth into the kingdom of God.

Seek Those Things Which Are Above!

"If then you were raised with Christ, seek those things which are above, where Christ is, sitting at the right hand of God. Set your mind on things above, not on things on the earth." (Colossians 3:1, 2)

It is only natural if we have been born from above to seek those things which are from above! This

Chapter 1: Born from Above!

makes perfect sense to me.

Now, the Apostle Paul makes a great observation here when he says, "If then you were raised with Christ."

What does this mean? It means that if you have surrendered your life to Christ and have now been raised or resurrected also with Christ, seek (or reach out) for those things which are above (heavenly things, ideas, concepts, principles, etc.) things that pertain to the plan of God and His Christ.

The second thing the Apostle Paul urges is to "set the mind on things above."

In this deep thought, what Paul is really pushing for is for the believer "to concentrate, to incline (ear)" towards heavenly thoughts or ideas.

Finally, Paul makes the clear-cut distinction be-

Chapter 1: Born from Above!

tween seeking things of heaven versus things on the earth. Things on the earth are things that pertain to the carnal man such as thoughts, ideas, philosophies, and concepts for self-aggrandizing.

It is the Apostle Paul's desire that the changed man would press into the affections of God by willful choice and not by force, guilt, or fear.

Remember, it was the things of earth that kept you and I in bondage, guilt, shame and disgrace. Paul suggests staying away from that realm.

Have You Lost Something?

Here's an interesting fact: When we lose touch with God or our freshness in the anointing of the Holy Spirit, when reading the Bible and spending time in personal prayer becomes difficult, or when spending time in worship before God, seems long and boring — then this is a sign, that

Chapter 1: Born from Above!

we have lost something!

Don't be deceived by your own heart [Obadiah 1:3] and don't be fooled by your own emotions [Psalm 103:1; 2 Samuel 12:20]. Both of these are contingent upon your willfulness to touch God.

You can align your heart with God's heart if you really want to, and you can bring your emotions under subjection as well. Remember: Your soul is not in charge, His Spirit is!

One sure sign that we have departed from His Spirit is our trend to want to be entertained. Instead of being lit by His fire, we look for a campfire! Instead of finding peace and joy in the Holy Spirit, we look for fun and games in a worldly spirit. As the late great Leonard Ravenhill one said, *"We only need entertainment when we have lost the joy of the Lord. If we have joy in the Lord, we don't need entertainment and if we don't have joy, we crave entertainment!"*

Chapter 1: Born from Above!

Being born from above is not something you intellectually think of doing; being born from above is something you step into! Either you are born from above or you are not!

Chapter 2

There Is Power in the Blood of Jesus!

If there is one thing that you must realize about your Christian experience this is it: You were born on a battlefield. This wonderful experience that has taken place within you is now being monitored in hell!

You must also realize that the Devil hates God's creations, and anything that God attempts to produce will be challenged by the powers of darkness.

What most believers don't realize is that the Devil is not playing games! He is not messing around with you to just give you a headache or make situations difficult for you.

My friends, the battle against the enemy is way more serious than this! Please understand that

Chapter 2: There Is Power in the Blood of Jesus!

the battle is real and on Satan's agenda his priority is to do everything in his power to shut down God's plan and purpose IN you and AROUND you!

It Happened in the Garden!

"So, He drove out the man; and He placed cherubim at the east of the garden of Eden, and a flaming sword which turned every way, to guard the way to the tree of life." (Genesis 3:24)

In chapter 3 of Genesis, we find the fall of man. This is the chapter that depicts the way man fell into sin before God. You have all read the story I'm sure. Now, when man sins, God immediately shows up. He calls man to account, and man is judged for the sins committed. This is the order of the Lord.

After Adam, Eve and the serpent are judged, God sends them out of the garden of Eden as an ad-

Chapter 2: There Is Power in the Blood of Jesus!

ditional form of judgment. He sends them out to figure out life on their own through their own ability and strength.

It is God's plan to restore man back to Himself and bring them back to the garden. The place that you could say is literally heaven on earth!

It is in the garden of Eden that man found his purpose for living. It was here where man recieved precious promises relating to eternal life, blessings, and prosperity forevermore, of course, until the serpent seduced mankind and all of God's plan came to a halt!

The garden of Eden is more than a geographical place, it's also a spiritual state that man arrives at through faith in Jesus Christ. Only by faith can someone understand and enter. In the New Testament, we call it the Kingdom of God.

The Life of Jesus Restores!

Chapter 2: There Is Power in the Blood of Jesus!

Knowing that Jesus came from heaven for the purpose of restoring man back to God (Eden) per se, Satan's plan then, was to stop man from reaching the door that would lead them there.

From the day of His birth, it was in the Devil's agenda to stop Jesus from carrying out His mission to set the world free from the power of sin and death.

In Matthew 4, the devil makes the attempt to trick Jesus into eating bread while He fasted. He also made the effort to get Jesus to jump off a pinnacle, and if that wasn't enough, the devil also tried to get Jesus to worship him. None of these methods and/or attempts to make Jesus disobey the Father's wishes worked!

Why did the devil attack Jesus so strongly? The attack was purposely made to make Jesus fall into the sin of disobedience, thus making His life impure before the Father, and if His life was impure, then Jesus would not be the perfect sacrifice for God. His life would be just like any other man, disqualified, and powerless to save!

The good news here is that Jesus didn't fall for the devil's tactics but rather overcame and became the Savior of the world. It was through His shed blood at the cross of Calvary that we found justification and acceptance before a Holy God. The blood made us clean and pure from all of our sin and ushered us back into the garden (of Eden).

The Power of the Blood

"For the life of the flesh is in the blood, and I have given it to you upon the altar to make atonement for your souls; for it is the blood that makes atonement for the soul." (Leviticus 17:11)

The blood of Jesus was shed for my life and because of His blood, I have entered into the kingdom of God as an overcomer! Listen to all the powerful benefits we get in His precious blood:

My Debt is Paid, Once and for All
"So Christ was offered once to bear the sins of many. To those who eagerly wait for Him He will appear a second time, apart from sin, for salvation." (Hebrews 9:28)

I Am Justified
"Much more then, having now been justified by His blood, we shall be saved from wrath through Him. " (Romans 5:9)

I Am Forgiven
"In Him we have redemption through His blood, the forgiveness of sins, according to the riches of His grace" (Ephesians 1:7)

I Am Spared from God's Wrath
"Much more then, having now been justified by His blood, we shall be saved from wrath through

Him. " (Romans 5:9)

I am being spiritually healed; one day even my flesh will be replaced with an incorruptible body.
". . . who Himself bore our sins in His own body on the tree, that we, having died to sin, might live for righteousness—by whose stripes you were healed." (I Peter 2:24)

I Am Spiritually Alive
"Then Jesus said to them, 'Most assuredly, I say to you, unless you eat the flesh of the Son of Man and drink His blood, you have no life in you.'" (John 6:53)

My judgment has been satisfied, and I am at peace with God
"But He was wounded for our transgressions, He was bruised for our iniquities; the chastisement for our peace was upon Him, and by His stripes we are healed." (Isaiah 53:5)

Chapter 2: There Is Power in the Blood of Jesus!

The bloodstream of His people Israel will be purged.
"For I will cleanse their blood that I have not cleansed: for the Lord dwells in Zion" (Joel 3:21)

I Am Cleansed
"But if we walk in the light as He is in the light, we have fellowship with one another, and the blood of Jesus Christ His Son cleanses us from all sin." (I John 1:7)

I Have the Power to Overcome the Enemy
"And they overcame him by the blood of the Lamb, and by the word of their testimony, and they loved not their lives unto the death." (Revelation 12:11)

I am no longer under the curse of the law
"Christ has redeemed us from the curse of the law, having become a curse for us (for it is written, 'Cursed is everyone who hangs on a tree'".) (Galatians 3:13)

Chapter 2: There Is Power in the Blood of Jesus!

I Have Been Reclaimed from the Enemy
"In Him we have redemption through His blood, the forgiveness of sins, according to the riches of His grace." (Ephesians 1:7)

I Am No Longer a Stranger to the Covenant of Promise.
". . . that at that time you were without Christ, being aliens from the commonwealth of Israel and strangers from the covenants of promise, having no hope and without God in the world. But now in Christ Jesus you who once were far off have been brought near by the blood of Christ." (Ephesians 2:12-13)

The Final Act of Public Expiation Has Been Made on my Behalf.
"For the life of a creature is in the blood, and I have given it to you to make atonement for yourselves on the altar; it is the blood that makes atonement for one's life." (Leviticus 17:11)

I have been moved from the enemy's kingdom into the kingdom of God

"Having disarmed principalities and powers, He made a public spectacle of them, triumphing over them in it." (Colossians 2:15)

I Have Gained the Unmerited Favor of God

"In Him we have redemption through His blood, the forgiveness of sins, according to the riches of His grace." (Ephesians 1:7)

I Have Been Declared Righteous

"For He made Him who knew no sin to be sin for us, that we might become the righteousness of God in Him." (2 Corinthians 5:21)

I Have Been Justified *(just as though I had never sinned)*

"...being justified freely by His grace through the redemption that is in Christ Jesus, whom God set forth as a propitiation by His blood, through faith, to demonstrate His righteousness, because in His forbearance God had passed over the sins that were previously committed." (Romans 3:24-25)

I Am Able to Come Close to God
"But now in Christ Jesus you who once were far off have been brought near by the blood of Christ." (Ephesians 2:13)

I Can Participate in the Sweet Communion of Remembrance of His Sacrifice
"Likewise, He also took the cup after supper, saying, 'This cup is the new covenant in My blood, which is shed for you.'" (Luke 22:20)

My Redemption Will Never Perish
"Knowing that you were not redeemed with corruptible things, like silver or gold, from your aimless conduct received by tradition from your fathers, but with the precious blood of Christ, as of a lamb without blemish and without spot." (1 Peter 1:18-19)

Chapter 2: There Is Power in the Blood of Jesus!

Jesus Testifies on My Behalf That I Am Clean

"...and from Jesus Christ, the faithful witness, the firstborn from the dead, and the ruler over the kings of the earth. To Him who loved us and washed us from our sins in His own blood and has made us kings and priests to His God and Father, to Him be glory and dominion forever and ever. Amen." (Revelation 1:5)

I Am Free

"Stand fast therefore in the liberty by which Christ has made us free, and do not be entangled again with a yoke of bondage." (Galatians 5:1)

I Am Protected from Judgment

"...that you shall say, 'It is the Passover sacrifice of the Lord, who passed over the houses of the children of Israel in Egypt when He struck the Egyptians and delivered our households.' So the people bowed their heads and worshiped." (Exodus 12:27)

Chapter 2: There Is Power in the Blood of Jesus!

I Am Freed from a Conscience Defiled by Guilt
"Let us draw near with a true heart in full assurance of faith, having our hearts sprinkled from an evil conscience and our bodies washed with pure water." (Hebrews 10:22)

I Am No Longer Condemned
"There is therefore now no condemnation to those who are in Christ Jesus, who do not walk according to the flesh, but according to the Spirit." (Romans 8:1)

I Have Been Separated from the World and Declared Holy *(wholly)* to God
"I have been crucified with Christ; it is no longer I who live, but Christ lives in me; and the life which I now live in the flesh I live by faith in the Son of God, who loved me and gave Himself for me." (Galatians 2:20)

I Can Proclaim Total Victory
"And they overcame him by the blood of the

Chapter 2: There Is Power in the Blood of Jesus!

Lamb, and by the word of their testimony, and they loved not their lives unto the death." (Revelation 12:11)

I Can Enter Boldly into the Holiest of Holiess and Live.

"Therefore, brethren, having boldness to enter the Holiest by the blood of Jesus, by a new and living way which He consecrated for us, through the veil, that is, His flesh, and having a High Priest over the house of God, let us draw near with a true heart in full assurance of faith, having our hearts sprinkled from an evil conscience and our bodies washed with pure water." (Hebrews 10:19-22)

I Have Further Revelation of Who God Is

"Who being the brightness of His glory and the express image of His person, and upholding all things by the word of His power, when He had by Himself purged our sins, sat down at the right hand of the Majesty on high." (Hebrews 1:3)

Chapter 2: There Is Power in the Blood of Jesus!

In closing this chapter, I want to bring before you that as we enter into Christ, we have everything to gain. We must by faith, appropriate ourselves of His precious blood and walk in its power!

Chapter 3

The Forgiven Life!

If there is one thing that we must realize about our life in God it is that our life is progressive.

We are continually progressing in the revelation of God and all that God desires to disclose to us as we become more intimate with Him.

Let us look at the different stages of spiritual maturity that God has brought before us by His great sacrifice on the cross of Calvary.

The believer must realize first and foremost, that they have been forgiven by God for all their sins—This is key to spiritual growth and maturity. Secondly, the believer must enter into the crucified life. This is a life of brokenness; the revelation that as a believer of Christ, we carry our cross. What does this mean? Carrying a cross

Chapter 3: The Forgiven Life!

is the understanding that our flesh is not going to rule over us anymore. By allowing Christ to hold first place in our lives, and by rendering the flesh powerless by willfully denying its desires, a crucified life is accomplished. All of this can be done by the power of the Holy Spirit that dwells richly within us.

The Apostle Paul realized this process of being crucified with Christ and living out a life of faith in Christ, just listen: "I have been crucified with Christ; it is no longer I who live, but Christ lives in me; and the life which I now live in the flesh, I live by faith in the Son of God, who loved me and gave Himself for me." (Galatians 2:20)

Finally, as we have crucified our flesh on the cross, we are to rise up to a life of fire in God. Our portion is to walk in resurrection power! Just as Jesus was raised from the dead, so are we to rise by the power of the Holy Spirit!

Chapter 3: The Forgiven Life!

This is what the word of God says, "Therefore we were buried with Him through baptism into death, that just as Christ was raised from the dead by the glory of the Father, even so we also should walk in newness of life. For if we have been united together in the likeness of His death, certainly we also shall be in the likeness of His resurrection." (Romans 6:4-5)

As we die to self and keep ourselves submitted to the Holy Spirit, the presence of God becomes more intense. This type of life will be marked by a life of brokenness and obedience to the will of God, bearing fruit everywhere it goes!

Let's look at it.

The Forgiven Life

"But if we walk in the light as He is in the light, we have fellowship with one another, and the blood of Jesus Christ His Son cleanses us from

Chapter 3: The Forgiven Life!

all sin. If we say that we have no sin, we deceive ourselves, and the truth is not in us. If we confess our sins, He is faithful and just to forgive us our sins and to cleanse us from all unrighteousness." (1 John 1:7-9)

Having understanding of the finished work of Christ is very important to the believer's faith. Without proper knowledge of what Christ has done for us, the believer is left with nothing but an empty religion full of ritualism and tradition.

For starters, Christ shed His blood on the cross at Calvary. He poured out His life as a ransom for all humanity. He didn't have to do it, but He did! No one could have forced Him to do it, He did it willfully!

The blood of Jesus cleanses us from our sins and justifies us before the Father. If we have been washed in the blood of Jesus, we have been forgiven for all the sins we have committed and our

Chapter 3: The Forgiven Life!

sins have been separated from us, as far as the east is from the west: "As far as the east is from the west, so far has He removed our transgressions from us." (Psalm 103:34)

Now, if our heart condemns us, let us bring it before Christ and wash in the blood – the blood is greater than whatever it is we are feeling: "But even if we don't feel at ease, God is greater than our feelings, and he knows everything." (1 John 3:20)

Also, the Scripture teaches us that, "There is therefore now no condemnation to those who are in Christ Jesus, who do not walk according to the flesh, but according to the Spirit." (Romans 8:1)

If anyone comes to accuse us of our past sins, then we have to apply the blood of Christ to that thought and say to that voice with absolute authority: "I have been justified by the blood of Je-

Chapter 3: The Forgiven Life!

sus and I am forgiven."

The Scripture also says that, it is appointed for man to die once and then comes the judgment— then know that Jesus met that appointment with death and defeated it. "And as it is appointed for men to die once, but after this the judgment, so Christ was offered once to bear the sins of many." (Hebrews 9:27-28).

So Death Has No Power Over Us!

There is only One that can judge us or condemn us— His name is Jesus! He said He would not do it [John 8:1].

Once we have entered into His plan and purpose by the blood of Jesus, no one can touch us. Listen to Paul's words here: "What then shall we say to these things? If God is for us, who can be against us? He who did not spare His own Son, but delivered Him up for us all, how shall

Chapter 3: The Forgiven Life!

He not with Him also freely give us all things? Who shall bring a charge against God's elect? It is God who justifies. Who is he who condemns? It is Christ who died, and furthermore is also risen, who is even at the right hand of God, who also makes intercession for us. Who shall separate us from the love of Christ? Shall tribulation, or distress, or persecution, or famine, or nakedness, or peril, or sword?
As it is written:

> *'For Your sake we are killed*
> *all day long;*
> *We are accounted as sheep*
> *for the slaughter.'*

Yet in all these things we are more than conquerors through Him who loved us. For I am persuaded that neither death nor life, nor angels, nor principalities, nor powers, nor things present nor things to come, nor height nor depth, nor any other created thing, shall be able to separate us from the love of God which is in Christ Jesus our Lord." (Romans 8:31-39)

We must know that we have been forgiven and set free by the blood of Jesus before we can move on to bigger and better things in God.

Chapter 4

The Crucified Life!

In the last chapter, *The Forgiven Life*, I alluded to the fact that God has forgiven us and there is no one that can judge us, apart from Him. This is who God the Father is, He is a forgiving Father!

We thank God for His only begotten Son, Jesus Christ, who paid the full price for our ransom and has brought us near to God through His shed blood on Calvary's cross. It is His sacrifice that made all the difference. It has transferred us from darkness to light— from a life of sin to a life of holiness.

Also, another worthy note is that Jesus called Himself the Door: "Then Jesus said to them again, 'Most assuredly, I say to you, I am the door of the sheep.'" (John 10:7)

Chapter 4: The Crucified Life!

Jesus said that He was the Door. Once you come in, you are entering His fold, His kingdom. It's a different world in His kingdom.

The kingdom of God has been made for a special kind of people, the redeemed of God. Those who have been bought with the price of blood, the blood of the Lamb. They are the only ones for whom this kingdom has been prepared.

Now as we have come into His kingdom, the next step is to grow in this kingdom. We are already in, and now it's time to grow in the knowledge of this kingdom. We will need to allow God, the Holy Spirit, to teach us about the King and His kingdom!

The Crucified Life

"I have been crucified with Christ; it is no longer I who live, but Christ lives in me; and the life which I now live in the flesh I live by faith in the

Chapter 4: The Crucified Life!

Son of God, who loved me and gave Himself for me." (Galatians 2:20)

Let me start by saying that the crucified life is not an easy life. As a matter of fact, it is impossible to live it without having been truly born-again.

Unless the Spirit of God comes in to teach us, there will be no learning taking place. We cannot learn the ways of God, the Father, without God, the Spirit!

It's a Willful Choice

Allowing God to become Lord of our life, is more of a willful choice, than God forcing us to join a religious experience, a club, or a ritual. If we don't step into the crucified life, then our lives remain the same. We will only have the knowledge that God saved us through His blood from sin, but we will never enter into His full experience. We will never know Him like God the Father intended for us to know Him!

In the book of John chapter 6, Jesus made a powerful comment. Listen to this: "Then Jesus said to them, 'Most assuredly, I say to you, unless you eat the flesh of the Son of Man and drink His blood, you have no life in you. Whoever eats My flesh and drinks My blood has eternal life, and I will raise him up at the last day. For My flesh is food indeed, and My blood is drink indeed. He who eats My flesh and drinks My blood abides in Me, and I in him. As the living Father sent Me, and I live because of the Father, so he who feeds on Me will live because of Me. This is the bread which came down from heaven—not as your fathers ate the manna and are dead. He who eats this bread will live forever.'" (John 6:53-58).

What Jesus in essence is saying, Look, if you eat of My flesh, and drink of my blood and if you participate in my death, you will know who I really am. As a matter of fact, it is the only way to abide

Chapter 4: The Crucified Life!

in Me, and I in you! You must allow me to enter you so you can enter Me! If you participate in Me — you will live forever.

The Cross is More Than Just a Symbol!

Here's what we must enter into today. We must understand that the cross of Christ is not only a symbol to hang as a necklace like some good luck charm; the cross of Christ is an instrument of death. It was made to hang criminals on—it's certainly not for good luck!

The words that the Apostle Paul used in Galatians 2:20 are very intentional and very powerful. We must grasp them so that we may understand the basis of the crucified life.

First of all, Paul understood that His life was no longer his— that is why the statement is made, "I have been crucified with Christ and I no longer live. But Christ lives in me."

Chapter 4: The Crucified Life!

Paul had made it clear to himself and to others, that his life as he knew it, no longer had any rights or dominion to do its own thing. His life now belonged to Christ. It was surrendered fully to the Lord's wishes, attitudes, thoughts, and actions. Paul was God -possessed!

In ancient times, someone carrying a cross was on the verge of being killed. As the man carried that cross outside the city walls, everyone knew that he was not coming back for his family. It was over for this man!

People would stare at him while he hung bleeding. People would make fun of him and birds would come and pluck out his eyes and bite him, etc. What was worse, was that this man no longer had the right to defend himself. He had been stripped of all rights and was now on the way to death.

Paul likens himself to a man carrying and dying

Chapter 4: The Crucified Life!

on a cross here. He is saying, When I gave my life to Jesus, I lost all my rights. I no longer have a life of my own, only what God allows me to have. I am a slave to Christ and will serve Him only. My goal, my plans, my desires, my vision, all of me – it all belongs to Christ now!

Do You See the Difference?

People who accept Jesus into their hearts so that they may find forgiveness for their sins, receive Him as Savior. Do you see this? We accept His free gift of forgiveness and we enter into His life and He enters ours. We exchange our filthy lives for His awesome life!

Many have thought that this is all there is in God. Are they so wrong!

Let me show you: Once we accept Jesus as Savior, His blood purifies us from our sins, and we can now stand before God, the Father. In other

Chapter 4: The Crucified Life!

words, the blood of Jesus has made us presentable before God. After this, the Lord desires to abide in us with His Holy Spirit and transform us into the image of Christ.

Before we can enter into Him, we must willfully accept the cross of Christ. The willingness to offer our whole self to follow Jesus must now take place. The cross of Christ will wipe away and bring under subjection the works of the flesh, which are found in us.

Paul puts it this way: "**. . . knowing this, that our old man was crucified with Him, that the body of sin might be done away with, that we should no longer be slaves of sin. For he who has died has been freed from sin.**" (Romans 6:6,7)

Do you want to be cleansed from your sins, and then get washed in the blood? Do you want to be a disciple of Jesus who impacts the world? Then go to the cross and be changed from your

Chapter 4: The Crucified Life!

old nature to His new nature!

The word Savior means someone who saves. The word Lord means someone who is the owner of all. We already accepted Him as Savior for He paid the price for our sins and we have received forgiveness— now it's time to make Him Lord. We are now ready to make Him owner of everything! Are you ready for this?

In closing, the crucified life is the continual surrendering of our fleshly attitudes, antics, thoughts, selfish ambitions, and desires to the Lord.. The crucified life leads us to a life of brokenness. It is this lifestyle that God desires from us. We will now be ready to be used by God as the resurrection power will flow unhindered from us!

Chapter 5

The Resurrected Life!

In following the progression of what God is doing in us through His Holy Spirit, and as we have crossed the sessions on *The Forgiven Life* and The Crucified Life, I will now turn your attention to *The Resurrected Life.*

In the resurrected life, it is important for the believer to know what has actually taken place in their spirit.

For one, the believer has been forgiven of all their sins, and secondly, the believer has entered into the death of Christ by taking their cross and denying themselves from their own desires to follow Christ wherever He goes! All these have been done by willful choice.

Also, it will be of great value, to know that once

Chapter 5: The Resurrected Life!

we have been crucified with Christ and we no longer live, but Christ lives in us; this new life that we are now living is sustained, and can only be sustained by faith. The resurrected life is a life of faith in God.

The resurrected life is a life of faith in the Son of God; it will manifest itself as one goes forth living out the experience that He has been risen from the dead and is now walking in the power of the resurrected Christ!

Let's look at it.

"And with great power the apostles gave witness to the resurrection of the Lord Jesus." (Acts 4:33)

As for the apostles of Christ in the early church, the message of the resurrected Christ could not be denied. The apostles had witnessed it and now they were full of the fire of God.

Chapter 5: The Resurrected Life!

I believe that this is one of the things that happens to people who have an encounter with the living Christ, they are vivified by His power. It is at this point that the experience is so overwhelmingly real, that it is impossible to stay quiet about this event in our lives!

The reason many people don't talk about their faith in Christ is because they haven't witnessed the power of God. They have heard about it, they might even have prayed about it, but they have not appropriated its power! It is not real to them, and if it is not real then it can't be shared. We can't give what we don't have! How can anyone witness something that they have not seen?

Let's go deeper:

"Therefore, we were buried with Him through baptism into death, that just as Christ was raised from the dead by the glory of the Father, even so we also should walk in newness of life. For if

Chapter 5: The Resurrected Life!

we have been united together in the likeness of His death, certainly we also shall be in the likeness of His resurrection, knowing this, that our old man was crucified with Him, that the body of sin might be done away with, that we should no longer be slaves of sin. For he who has died has been freed from sin. Now if we died with Christ, we believe that we shall also live with Him, knowing that Christ, having been raised from the dead, dies no more. Death no longer has dominion over Him. For the death that He died, He died to sin once for all; but the life that He lives, He lives to God. Likewise, you also, reckon yourselves to be dead indeed to sin, but alive to God in Christ Jesus our Lord." (Romans 6:4-11)

Let me bring out two important elements from these few verses.

"Christ was raised from the dead by the glory of the Father, even so we also should walk in newness of life."

Chapter 5: The Resurrected Life!

Here is an important fact: We have been raised to walk in newness of life. What is the newness of life? The newness of life denotes a life that is filled with new longings, new desires, new passions, new dreams, new ambitions, etc.

2 Corinthians 5:17 says, "Therefore, if anyone is in Christ, he is a new creation; old things have passed away; behold, all things have become new."

This particular Scripture says that we are a new creation. In other words, the thing created had not existed before. What God has made out of you and I in this new birth, has never been seen before. Old things, meaning everything in the past has been done away with; and now, all things have become new. To become new means that those things have never existed before, but they are about to manifest through us. Likewise, you also, reckon yourself to be dead indeed to sin, but alive to God!

Chapter 5: The Resurrected Life!

In walking-out the resurrected life that God has given us, we reckon or consider ourselves dead to the life of sin. We no longer have that taskmaster of sin to order us around. We have been set free from his grip! In other words, we don't have to sin.

The truth of the matter is the following: God has made us come alive for him! By the power of His Holy Spirit, God has made us come alive or vivified our spirit, soul, and body to serve Him. Do you see this?

It is no longer us who live but Christ who lives in us! We are now able to do all that Christ did on the earth where He was rejected. This is why we were quickened by His Spirit – so that we might live in the power of God to do the works of God.

The Devil Hates the Resurrection!

"Now while they were going, behold, some of

Chapter 5: The Resurrected Life!

the guards came into the city and reported to the chief priests all the things that had happened. When they had assembled with the elders and consulted together, they gave a large sum of money to the soldiers, saying, 'Tell them, "His disciples came at night and stole Him away while we slept." And if this comes to the governor's ears, we will appease him and make you secure.' So they took the money and did as they were instructed; and this saying is commonly reported among the Jews until this day." (Matthew 28:11-15)

If there is something that I know the devil would love to discredit, it has to be the reality of the resurrection of Jesus! How would he love to rewrite history and say that Jesus never resurrected from the grave! Too bad— HE DID!

For years the truth about Christ resurrecting in bodily form has been under attack by other religions, agnostics, and all kinds of devil-minded

Chapter 5: The Resurrected Life!

people.

The fact that Christ resurrected means that He is alive! If Christ is alive, then everything He told us is true, and we are no longer in our sins. Furthermore, Christ is now multiplied into the hearts of all who believe in Him and made Him Lord of their lives.

God's Holy Spirit has been sent down from heaven to live in our hearts forevermore and to teach us the mind of God.

The benefit of being resurrected in our hearts by the Holy Spirit and to walk in power and in full authority, is ever present.

No wonder the devil hates the resurrection of Jesus— no wonder he does all in his power to discredit what Christ did to the tomb! Now we who believe in Christ are giving witness to this great power by manifesting His presence in every place where two or three gather in His Name!

Signs and Wonders!

Listen to this: "And these signs will follow those who believe: In My name they will cast out demons; they will speak with new tongues; they will take up serpents; and if they drink anything deadly, it will by no means hurt them; they will lay hands on the sick, and they will recover." (Mark 16:17, 18)

You and I are called to do signs and wonders. The Scripture says that those who follow Christ will do them. Due to the resurrection power of Jesus working in us, we are able to experience signs and wonders.

Not only was Jesus resurrected from the grave; we were resurrected from our flesh— we walk in Christ's power now!

Chapter 5: The Resurrected Life!

Is it any wonder to you why the devil fights us when we are resurrected? Does it make you wonder why the devil hates us so much when we draw near to Christ? He wants to instill fear, condemnation, guilt, shame, and doubt upon you by means of our flesh.

That is why dying to self is so essential— for the resurrection power is contingent upon our spiritual death to the flesh first. Unless we die to self and resurrect in Christ's power, we will not be able to live for God. Now, if we do come alive— devil watch out!

Chapter 6

Branded by the Lord!

"Are they Hebrews? So am I. Are they Israelites? So am I. Are they the seed of Abraham? So am I. Are they ministers of Christ?—I speak as a fool—I am more: in labors more abundant, in stripes above measure, in prisons more frequently, in deaths often. From the Jews five times I received forty stripes minus one. Three times I was beaten with rods; once I was stoned; three times I was shipwrecked; a night and a day I have been in the deep; in journeys often, in perils of waters, in perils of robbers, in perils of my own countrymen, in perils of the Gentiles, in perils in the city, in perils in the wilderness, in perils in the sea, in perils among false brethren; in weariness and toil, in sleeplessness often, in hunger and thirst, in fastings often, in cold and nakedness—besides the other things, what comes upon me daily: my deep concern for all

Chapter 6: Branded by the Lord!

the churches. Who is weak, and I am not weak? Who is made to stumble, and I do not burn with indignation? If I must boast, I will boast in the things which concern my infirmity. The God and Father of our Lord Jesus Christ, who is blessed forever, knows that I am not lying. In Damascus the governor, under Aretas the king, was guarding the city of the Damascenes with a garrison, desiring to arrest me; but I was let down in a basket through a window in the wall, and escaped from his hands." (2 Corinthians 11:11-33)

When the Lord touches our life, it is inevitable that a big change will take place. There will be a powerful transformation in our ideas and attitudes about life altogether. When God touches our life, we will manifest a life of faith and full confidence in who God is and what He can do in us and through us!

The Apostle Paul was faced with much opposition and in spite of all this, he never gave up! As a matter of fact, his attitude was that of an overcomer. He felt that he was called to make a difference during his lifetime; the Apostle Paul was fully convinced that nothing or no one, would hinder the flow of God in and through his life!

Paul felt a great debt toward the lost, he felt the burden to preach the gospel to them that they may be saved. He was not shy, timid, or scared of what man could do to him.

How many of us live with this type of attitude and conviction of heart? How many of us feel in debt to the lost? How many of us are willing to step out of our comfort zone and make an advancement for the kingdom of God?

Branded for Jesus!

"From now on let no person trouble me (by making it necessary for me to vindicate my apostolic authority and the divine truth of my Gospel) for I

Chapter 6: Branded by the Lord!

bear on my body the (brand) marks of the Lord Jesus (the wounds, scars, and other outward evidence of persecutions—these testify to His ownership of me)!" (Galatians 6:17, 18)

Paying the price for serving King Jesus is not an easy thing to do. Serving the Lord with all our heart is not a religious duty, and it can't be done by willpower alone! Serving Jesus comes by experiencing revelation in our inner-man; it will require our mind, our heart, our soul, and all our strength to walk in the will of the Father.

Too many people struggle in their dedication to the Lord when it really counts. Anyone can sing songs and praise the Lord when things are going well and dandy! I wonder seriously, how many believers can worship the Lord in the midst of a chaotic experience? How many can keep flowing in God's fire when everything in hell is trying to extinguish their fire? My friends, let us reflect on this!

Chapter 6: Branded by the Lord!

Are You Concerned About You?

In living out this gospel, there is no room for you! You can't be worried about you and worried about God's will. It's either you offer yourself to the Lord fully and allow Him to rule and reign in your emotions, your thoughts and actions or struggle day in and day out with outward situations, circumstances, and adversities.

It is no fun in trying to keep up with God's agenda as well as our own agenda. Life will be difficult no matter how you slice it! Either it will be the Lord who will meet and take care of all our needs, or it will be us, making countless feeble efforts to make our own plans, dreams, and ambitions come to pass.

Paul's attitude here to the Galatian church was one of I know what I believe and in whom I trust, so stop trying to show me something different! Paul was trying to make it clear that he had paid

Chapter 6: Branded by the Lord!

a hefty price for serving Jesus and that he had the marks (he calls them branding) of the countless times he was beaten and left for dead— all for the sake of Christ!

When we have walked with God in total devotion, we have nothing and no one to fear! The Lord has always come first (in our lives) in the past, is coming first today, and will always be first as long as we live. Nothing can move us, shake us, or convince us otherwise. This is the heart of those who have been branded for the Lord. Do you see the blessing behind the branding?

You Can't Run Scared!

"Now when we heard these things, both we and those from that place pleaded with him not to go up to Jerusalem. Then Paul answered, 'What do you mean by weeping and breaking my heart? For I am ready not only to be bound, but also to die at Jerusalem for the name of the Lord Jesus.'"

Chapter 6: Branded by the Lord!

(Acts 21:12, 13)

When I read this particular scene where the Apostle Paul is warned by some disciples to not go to Jerusalem for his own good, I can truly see the sincere concern that his friends had for him. They were afraid for Paul's life, and with reason. Yet Paul was not afraid!

When will the church get it? When will we realize that a man who has died to self, is not afraid to be bound or to die for the sake of Christ!

If we are going to live for Jesus, let us live for Jesus! Let us stop making excuses for why we are not more dedicated. We need to stop making excuses for why we don't pray, why we don't fast, and why we can't spend a few minutes in God's word in deep meditation!

Any form of advancement of the good news of the gospel of the kingdom, will be met head on

Chapter 6: Branded by the Lord!

by Satan and his demons! Franklin Hall said it this way, *"We shall always have to fight for the proper way to live!"* Get ready to fight!

Chapter 7

Are You Making Yourself Available?

"A certain woman of the wives of the sons of the prophets cried out to Elisha, saying, 'Your servant my husband is dead, and you know that your servant feared the Lord. And the creditor is coming to take my two sons to be his slaves.'

So, Elisha said to her, 'What shall I do for you? Tell me, what do you have in the house?'

And she said, 'Your maidservant has nothing in the house but a jar of oil.'

Then he said, 'Go, borrow vessels from everywhere, from all your neighbors—empty vessels; do not gather just a few. And when you have come in, you shall shut the door behind you and your sons; then pour it into all those vessels and set aside the full ones.'

So, she went from him and shut the door behind her and her sons, who brought the vessels to her; and she poured it out. Now it came to pass,

Chapter 7: Are You Making Yourself Available?

when the vessels were full, that she said to her son, 'Bring me another vessel.'
And he said to her, 'There is not another vessel.' So, the oil ceased." (2 Kings 4:1-6)

When I first came into the kingdom of God and knew in my heart that God had truly forgiven me of all my sins, not just some, but all sins; I burned deep with desire to serve Him. Now, I was shy and quiet and didn't want to express any of those emotions, so I never said anything to anyone—but God knew my heart!

Some time after being saved, I joined a church. It was at this place that my passion to serve Jesus grew. My pastor would challenge us to not only love God, but to serve Him with single-hearted devotion.

I still remember the feeling I would get when my pastor would challenge us with words that made us feel like if we were not serving God, then we

Chapter 7: Are You Making Yourself Available?

were not walking according to His will.

Week after week, our hearts were challenged, and many hearts were changed. Some were called to the mission field, and they went; others were called to open local ministries, and they went!

It was definitely a time of growing in the revelation of what it meant to make ourselves available for the Lord's use. I thank God for those glorious experiences and challenges.

It was not long after being bombarded by convicting messages, that the Lord chose me to follow His heart into the work of ministry. Handpicked by the Lord, I proceeded to make the necessary changes that would facilitate for me to leave secular work and pursue my King in His service.

It's been over thirty years now, and I still keep

Chapter 7: Are You Making Yourself Available?

wishing God had called me much earlier.

Being called by the Lord is not the easiest thing in the world. Actually, it is probably the hardest thing for any American to do. Being full of multiple blessings and opportunities to pursue the American Dream, many don't even take the time to align themselves with the voice of the Holy Spirit to find out what it is exactly what the Lord wants from them.

I remember hearing this hymn at one service. I will never forget the burning passion for Jesus that so overtook me and transformed my philosophy of life:

Hear the Lord of Harvest Sweetly Calling,
Who Will Go and Work For Me To-Day?
Who Will Bring To Me The Lost And Dying?
Who Will Point Them To The Narrow Way?

Speak, My Lord, Speak to Me,

Chapter 7: Are You Making Yourself Available?

Speak, And I'll Be Quick to Answer Thee;
Speak, My Lord, Speak to Me,
Speak, And I Will Answer, Lord, Send Me.

When the Coal of Fire Touched The Prophet,
Making Him As Pure, As Pure Can Be,
When The Voice Of God Said, Who'll Go For Us?
Then He Answered, Here I Am, Send Me.

Millions Now in Sin and Shame Are Dying;
Listen To Their Sad And Bitter Cry;
Hasten, Brother, Hasten To The Rescue;
Quickly Answer, Master, Here Am I.

Soon the Time for Reaping Will Be Over;
Soon We'll Gather For The Harvest-Home;
May The Lord Of Harvest Smile Upon Us,
May We Hear His Blessed Child, Well Done!

It is with this very passion I write this chapter today.

Chapter 7: Are You Making Yourself Available?

A Crossroad Experience

The story begins with a widow who lost her husband who died with some serious debt. After passing away, the creditors came looking for payment. Being that the woman had no money to pay, the creditor told her that he would take the children as payment.

There is nothing like a good test in our lives to get us to the place where God wants us to be; plus nothing tests our faith like a fiery furnace!

I have discovered that the opportunity to make a move for God, doesn't usually come when everything is fine and dandy. As a matter of fact, our emotions may even be at an all-time low, when the Lord comes calling! This happened to this woman— God called her to make a move while under extreme duress!

What Can We Offer God?

Chapter 7: Are You Making Yourself Available?

When the woman approached the Prophet, who represented the voice of God, he heard her need, "Elisha said to her, 'What shall I do for you? Tell me, what do you have in the house?'"

These are the ways of God! He will hear our needs and concerns first, then He will ask us what we want Him to do. Whether we answer or not, He will still question us with, "What do you have in your house?"

This question will change everything!

Does the Lord really need anything to make something happen? Well of course He doesn't need anything! Yet, he will always use what little we do have. He wants to be connected with us in some way and partner with us. God is all about cooperation. As usual, He expects us to do the natural, and He will do the supernatural!

The Secret to Miracles

Chapter 7: Are You Making Yourself Available?

The Lord, through Elisha, gives her instructions; these are words that if followed, would bring forth great fruit. The Prophet said to her, "Go, borrow vessels from everywhere, from all your neighbors—empty vessels; do not gather just a few. And when you have come in, you shall shut the door behind you and your sons; then pour it into all those vessels and set aside the full ones."

Many have often wondered at what time miracles happen, or in general, when do miracles actually take place? I have studied His word and have discovered that most miracles take place when one immediately obeys!

As she went, God began working on her miracle of multiplying the little amount of oil she still had in a jar.

There Is Not Another Vessel

"Now it came to pass, when the vessels were

full, that she said to her son, 'Bring me another vessel.'
And he said to her, 'There is not another vessel.'
So, the oil ceased."

As I close this chapter, I want you to see something very deep here. God instructed the widow what to do with her jar of oil, the borrowed vessels, and told her when borrowed vessels would be filled. He didn't tell her what to do once all the vessels were full! Why not?

This speaks of our own lives and how God operates in His kingdom.

So long as we continue offering ourselves to God as empty vessels, He will fill us. Once we say that we are full, His oil will cease! We must continually offer ourselves to be full of God, but there is a catch to this, we must also give away what God has deposited within!

Chapter 7: Are You Making Yourself Available?

I often hear people cry out for more of His presence or more of Jesus. I have come to know that most of the people who do the loud boisterous crying out for more, are the ones who never do anything for God!

My belief and it's only my opinion— unless we can justify our thirst and our calling it out for more, we should not be asking for more!

Chapter 8

The Ministry of Brokenness!

I would like to start my chapter on the Ministry of Brokenness by saying that this ministry is perhaps, one of the most misunderstood ministries ever. The ministry of brokenness is a ministry of surrender, pure devotion, and self-sacrificing for the sake of Christ.

The opposite of a ministry of brokenness, would probably be a message that propagates blessing without following principle, a resurrection without having to die first, prosperity without spiritual ascendency, and reaping without sowing!

As I share the value of brokenness, some people shy away from it. I have spoken to brothers and sisters in Christ, to pastors and leaders, to five-fold ministers, etc. to embrace the ministry that Jesus walked-out so powerfully, here on

Chapter 8: The Ministry of Brokenness!

earth where He was rejected by traditional religion, selfish followers, and sleepy disengaged disciples.

What is it about the ministry of brokenness that makes it so unattractive to Christians in general? Why the rejection of this divine-ordered lifestyle? I have heard some believers say that the ministry of brokenness is really a negative view of what it means to walk with Jesus. I beg to differ!

One time I heard an individual say, "If Jesus already paid the price for me; why should I have to pay any price? I should be having fun, fun, fun!"

As childish as this point of view sounds, many movements have embraced it. The self-help gospel, the name it and claim it gospel, the prosperity gospel, and now the user-friendly gospel, to name a few.

Let me just say this and get it off my chest: Peo-

Chapter 8: The Ministry of Brokenness!

ple who don't like the ministry of brokenness are probably people who don't understand what the ministry of brokenness really is! I know the ministry of brokenness sends chills down the spine of every carnal Christian— they tend to wiggle and dance around it, but all to no avail. Let God be true and every man a liar!

God is calling us to a ministry that brings about His power, His presence, and His purpose!

Christ the Pattern of Brokenness

"Then Jesus said to them, 'When you lift up the Son of Man, then you will know that I am He, and that I do nothing of Myself; but as My Father taught Me, I speak these things. And He who sent Me is with Me. The Father has not left Me alone, for I always do those things that please Him.'" (John 8:28-29)

Let me start by saying that the ministry of bro-

Chapter 8: The Ministry of Brokenness!

kenness was exemplified by Christ when He affirmed His relationship with the Father, and confirmed that His whole intent for being here on earth was to please Him.

Jesus was very clear about what made His life complete— completeness came when He obeyed. He never spent time alone apart from the Father. Jesus was sold on the idea that the Father was the leader, and He followed the Father's heart and wishes.

Because Jesus was a man who followed the Father and the Father could fully trust Him, Jesus would only speak and teach what the Father would deposit into Him. No wonder Jesus said, "I do nothing of Myself."

He was being led every step of the way!

Furthermore, Jesus said, "The Father has not left Me alone."

Chapter 8: The Ministry of Brokenness!

How was Jesus so sure of this? Where did He get this kind of confidence to speak out as boldly as He did? Well, Jesus was convinced that He was never alone. Why did He feel so close to God? Here's the answer: Jesus said, "I always do those things that please Him."

Setting Your Heart from the Start!

When you know what Christ is in you, and how He desires to govern and direct your steps in life has become a reality to you, then you will not want to do anything on your own without His leadership.

If we set our hearts to always do those things that please Him as a lifetime priority first, then we will never be left alone.

Very Costly Oil

"And being in Bethany at the house of Simon the

Chapter 8: The Ministry of Brokenness!

leper, as He sat at the table, a woman came having an alabaster flask of very costly oil of spikenard. Then she broke the flask and poured it on His head." (Mark 14:3)

In this story, we find a woman who had a very expensive flask of costly spikenard. Typically, no one just pulls that out for any occasion. This perfume was usually used for a woman's wedding day. So, it was not only expensive, but also reserved for a very special day in a woman's life.

When she saw Jesus, she broke the flask and poured all the oil that was in it on the head of Jesus! Wow. What does this show you and I? It shows us that it doesn't matter how expensive the outer flask is, it must be broken first, before we can pour it out on anyone.

In this case, Jesus was the recipient of this costly oil.

Chapter 8: The Ministry of Brokenness!

Had the woman said, I want to give my most costly perfume to Jesus, but I don't want to break the flask, then pouring oil on Christ's head would be nearly impossible!

God is calling us to break our flesh, so that His spirit can flow through us and into a world that needs the sweet-smelling aroma of the love of Christ!

What Does Jesus Think of the Breaking?

"But there were some who were indignant among themselves, and said, 'Why was this fragrant oil wasted? For it might have been sold for more than three hundred denarii and given to the poor.' And they criticized her sharply. But Jesus said, 'Let her alone. Why do you trouble her? She has done a good work for Me.' (Mark 14:4-6)

It's interesting to me how much the devil hates

Chapter 8: The Ministry of Brokenness!

the ministry of brokenness! The enemy will use anything in his power to prevent us from being broken for Christ. He will instill fear, doubt, unbelief, etc.

He will make any believer think twice about letting go of his life and trusting Jesus fully with it. He will replay repeatedly and make you dwell on how much you will lose if you give yourself fully to obey the Lord and deny yourself!

The enemy will always give you other (fleshly) ideas so that we may be supportive of others without having to give away our most costly commodities, gifts, or sacrifices!

The Enemy Knows!

As I close this chapter, please hear my heart on this: The enemy knows what is coming and trembles. It is time you also knew and realized what is coming!

Chapter 8: The Ministry of Brokenness!

The enemy knows that if we were ever to wake-up to this reality of being broken, and being poured out, the enemy knows he is done!

Don't cooperate with the enemy by loving your life more than you love Jesus! That is what the enemy wants. Allow God to break you and use you for His glory!

Chapter 9

The Gift of Faith Unleashed!

In this chapter, I would like to bring forth the element that makes God so real to the human heart, not to mention the connection we can have with Him to do supernatural acts in the world we live in.

In many Christian circles today, even on mainline denominations, the gift of faith is talked about and preached about, but to be honest with you, it comes with a powerless view of what God can do through His servants.

In other cases, the gift of faith is taken into another extreme, an opposite extreme. For example, in many charismatic circles, I have seen believers trying to name and claim things that are not there!

Chapter 9: The Gift of Faith Unleashed!

When an attempt is made to bring some correction to some of these extreme views of faith and sensationalism that accompanies them, it offends people. Some people have created doctrines out of one-time experiences or worse yet, they have created dogmatic views on the subject of faith by taking Scripture out of context.

As a servant of the Lord, and as one who longs, even yearns, to be used by God in supernatural ways, let me share my view on the gift of faith.

Faith Is!

"NOW FAITH is the assurance (the confirmation, the title deed) of the things (we) hope for, being the proof of things (we) do not see and the conviction of their reality (faith perceiving as real fact what is not revealed to the senses)." (Hebrews 11:1 -Amplified Bible)

Too often we have read this one verse in Hebrews

Chapter 9: The Gift of Faith Unleashed!

11:1, and simply figure that faith is either a supernatural emotion that comes upon the believer to do supernatural things, or faith is something so divine and so out there, that only a selected few attain this kind of faith.

Wow. A Title Deed!

Here's a bit of what I have experienced in walking in the power of God. When it comes to faith and the impartation of it, yes, a title deed is a figurative illustration of what faith is likened to.

When the Lord speaks to us, whether through a prophetic dream or word, or even through a prophet of God, the transfer of that word must be done as a transaction of a thing or a promise.

This promise has a title deed attached to it. If God tells you that you are receiving a new car in about a year, and along with that promise you will receive the assurance or confidence deep in

Chapter 9: The Gift of Faith Unleashed!

your spirit that it will happen—then it will happen! In other words, God just gave you the title deed to that promise. It is going to come to pass.

The Faith that Comes from God!

"Now in the morning, as they passed by, they saw the fig tree dried up from the roots. And Peter, remembering, said to Him, 'Rabbi, look! The fig tree which You cursed has withered away.' So Jesus answered and said to them, 'Have faith in God. For assuredly, I say to you, whoever says to this mountain, Be removed and be cast into the sea, and does not doubt in his heart, but believes that those things he says will be done, he will have whatever he says.'" (Mark 11:20-23)

In these verses in Mark, we find Jesus performing another miracle, this time the drying up of a fig tree. Jesus cursed this tree the evening before, and it dried up overnight. To this Peter was amazed and said, "Rabbi, look! The fig tree

Chapter 9: The Gift of Faith Unleashed!

which You cursed has withered away."

To Peter's comment Jesus simply replied: "Have faith in God."

The correct rendition in its original manuscripts means to have the faith OF God, not IN God. This exchange of words makes all the difference in the world!

Many scholars believe that when the word was translated from its original writings, the real context got lost in its translation into the English language. Therefore, it is inaccurate to say, "Have faith IN God." The correct wording should be, "Have faith OF God."

So what Jesus is literally saying here is, Peter, have the faith OF God in you, and you will move mountains. If you don't doubt in your heart but believe the things you say will be done, you will have whatever you say.

Chapter 9: The Gift of Faith Unleashed!

Now, the faith OF God comes from God alone!

Don't get the idea of going around and confessing that God gave you something, when, in reality, God never told you a darn thing! To believe something by repeatedly talking yourself into it, is nothing more than a metaphysical type of faith. It's a fleshly, soulish, or carnal type of faith— it was born inside of you by your own genius and not the Holy Spirit. This type of faith is not the faith OF God. This is selfish faith usually used for personal gain.

The faith of God is unique in that it is God who gives it to you. When God decides to heal someone through you, He will release this faith into you and you will go in His Name and heal the sick individual, without error. They will know that it was God who stepped into the room and performed the miracle!

You Know that You Know!

Chapter 9: The Gift of Faith Unleashed!

"Faith comes by hearing and hearing a word from God." (Romans 10:17)

In moving in the gift of faith, one must always be attentive to the many devices that the enemy uses to trick even the most anointed children of God. Now, the Scripture I want to use to further open your understanding on the subject is this one here, "Faith comes by hearing and hearing a word from God."

Faith is awakened when it hears the voice of God, a word from God. Anytime the Spirit of God connects with your own spirit, faith is activated by God's words. It's electrifying!

When God speaks to our heart, we know that we know, that it is God's word! There is a spiritual transfer that takes place when God speaks; it is almost as if we were receiving a title deed to some land or car! Our next step would be to obey the instruction, as it has been laid out by the Holy Spirit.

Watch Out with Presumption!

Before closing this chapter of faith, let me just say this: Let us not be calling faith something that faith is not! Let us be watchful that we don't step out by faith and fall into a deep pit of sorrow, all because we didn't obey the Holy Spirit. As a matter of fact, we were only obeying ourselves for the sake of our own convenience!

Let us not call everything as from God until we truly know that our experience of faith did come from God and not from us. Let us not be found guilty in accommodating our lifestyle for our own convenience and gain and dare say, Jesus told me!

There is a lot of presumption replacing real faith. Presumption is something we try to reason into existence while true faith is given only by God to

Chapter 9: The Gift of Faith Unleashed!

the inner man. We, as human beings, are very intelligent and therefore feel that our common sense is always correct.

In real faith, our hearts are the recipients. Once our inner man gets a hold of what God spoke to it, mountains will move, yes, miracles will manifest!

Always remember: Real faith can only come from God and deposited by God into our Spirit.

Chapter 10

Megaton Power!

"But you shall receive power when the Holy Spirit has come upon you; and you shall be witnesses to Me in Jerusalem, and in all Judea and Samaria, and to the end of the earth." (Acts 1:9)

To be a mighty force for God in the world we live in, His power must be present in you. It is not enough to just be saved— we need something more powerful than words or an experience; we need the power of God within and flowing out from us to the world!

Unless one is willing to be a witness (which in Greek the word translates to martyr) and willing to die for the cause of Christ, one will always struggle to please God on any level.

We must always be willing to please God. Re-

Chapter 10: Megaton Power!

member: He is not only our Savior but also our Lord and King. We who believe, are part of a kingdom that cannot be shaken!

In your prayer times, always make it a point to ask God to fill you with His Spirit and with the evidence of speaking in other tongues. Why not be filled with all that God has for you? God knew that you and I would need all His gifts to wage the good warfare.

The Power of Fasting and Prayer

I recently spent forty days fasting and praying. What was I looking for? Why the sacrifice? Why pay such a high price of denying myself the delicacies of common life and lending myself to the Lord at such a high level? Why would anyone want to fast for such a long time?

These are all questions I asked myself, as I gave myself to prayer and fasting for these many days.

Chapter 10: Megaton Power!

It was a great challenge to say the least, but let me tell you, going without food for forty days, is not an easy thing to do. As a matter of fact, daily, I would fight off the temptation to get back to regular life and just forget the fast.

Missing the sweet fellowship with God's people, missing out on birthday cakes, missing out on delicious breakfast, lunches, and dinners with fellow friends to name a few things, would challenge me. The desire to go back to regular life and just enjoy the rich blessing of God and live under His grace and favor sounded so much better.

It is easy to justify why we should not fast.

We can always find one hundred reasons why we should not fast or fast when the Lord tells us to do it. All these excuses are good, but will these excuses fill you with God's power?

Chapter 10: Megaton Power!

A Godly Motivation: Hungry for More!

Here are things that I am very grateful for: I am grateful for people who speak the prophetic word with accuracy, for the servants of God who pray for the sick and see results, for the gifted apostles who set up government and established new churches, for the teacher who researches God's word and teaches with accuracy the full council of God, for the evangelist who still believes that the gospel of the good news is still the answer for this fallen world.

Among the things that I am grateful for are the servants of the Lord who serve in the local church by loving and praying for each other, for the love that is shared among them, for the care and concern for the sick, the drug addict, the orphan, and the widow.

I am filled with gratitude for the revivalist from the past and for all those who are now praying

Chapter 10: Megaton Power!

for a mighty revival of His glory upon our nation and the world. Yes, my heart is grateful for all the moves of God I have been able to experience in my lifetime so far, but...

I am hungry for so much more in my life! I know my life has been called for so much more, and I will not be denied all that God has prepared for me.

Whether my life is bruised and beaten by life's woes, trials, adversities, atrocities, challenges, attacks, or whatever the case may be— I will be God's watchmen! Even if I have to stand bruised and beaten on my post, I will not leave my post! I refuse to quit! I will not be denied!

Jesus will receive the reward of His sufferings through my life! Come what may, I serve the devil notice: I will not leave my post!

Time to Possess Your Assignment!

Chapter 10: Megaton Power!

In the book, *The Fasting Prayer* by Franklin Hall, which in my humble opinion, is one of the best books I have read about fasting and prayer, the Holy Spirit taught me something very valuable. This is what the Spirit of God said to me: You will always have to fight for the right way to live!

It is time to realize that you and I were born for an assignment. God planned something out and then chose you and me. You and I are God's vessels to do His assignment.

Now, we can do that assignment by our own strength, wisdom, and ability, or we can enter the assignment with humility and plead with God for the megaton power that comes only from Him to carry it out!

Many people do great projects; they accomplish great exploits using what they have. If those people feel good about themselves for doing it their own way— good for them! This much I know,

Chapter 10: Megaton Power!

God's assignment must be done God's way. As the Scripture says, "So he answered and said to me, 'This is the word of the LORD to Zerubbabel: Not by might nor by power, but by My Spirit,' Says the LORD of hosts." (Zechariah 4:6)

People who understand that God has given them an assignment, do everything in their power to align themselves with God's wishes. They make all the necessary changes so that they may be ready should He call and send them to possess the land!

My View on Fasting and Prayer

Now my view on fasting and prayer may not be the same as yours. I have read countless books on the subject, and some I agree with and some I discard. They range from abusing your body with fasting for endless periods of time so that God can be pleased, to fasting and praying for God to grant you what you want.

Chapter 10: Megaton Power!

My philosophy on fasting is very simple: No food for twenty-four hours constitutes one day of fasting. You decide how many days you want to do this. I don't fast to get something (a miracle, a car, a house, a healing, a breakthrough, etc.) from the Lord; I fast so that my flesh is brought under subjection to the voice of God. Once I hear God's instruction, I can obey it and see results, just as God promised! I have never been into twisting God's arm to give me what I want or need. It sounds funny, but this is exactly what the church at large does! We should only fast to get God's mind and heart on the situation at hand!

What Is this Megaton Power?

The results of a life of fasting and prayer are immense. The rewards for dying to self and lending yourself to be set on fire by the Spirit of God is very powerful. Does God really need my fast to do His will? Obviously, the answer is no! But

Chapter 10: Megaton Power!

we need the exercise of fasting because of natural tendencies to fall into the works of the flesh. The seduction to fall into mediocrity, the allurement to pursue earthly dreams, the temptation to transgress God's commands, and the weakness to please yourself, more than God, is evermore present! Yes, we need to fast more than we think!

As we fast from food, we are literally denying ourselves; we are starving our flesh and bringing it into a powerless state. Also, one thing to note as we fast—we will feel the weakness in our body due to the lack of nourishment. Headaches also will accompany a fast most of the time. Don't be alarmed. Just keep pressing on— the headaches will eventually subside, and the weakness will subside as we find strength in God.

The prayer fast is not only denying ourselves from food— we must also seek God in prayer and in His word. These exercises will lift the spirit-man

Chapter 10: Megaton Power!

up to God and bring us before His presence.

If we fast without prayer, then the results are only weight loss. If we fast from food and include a time of prayer and meditation in God's word, we will be positioning ourselves to receive greater revelations from the Lord, and the power to obey God at much higher levels. As we obey God under this unction, God's power will accompany us in greater ways.

My encounters with God have been deeply enriched by protracted fasts. I have been to the heavenlies countless times and have experienced the realm of God in ways I had never seen. A greater understanding of His assignment for my life has been revealed, cleared up and expanded. Visitations from the Lord, angels, and demon power have also taken place. Prophetic dreams, divine appointments, and connections have been presented also. There have also been many things that God has not allowed me to share, but you will discover many things as you make your way through a protracted fast, of this you can be sure!

Chapter 11

Have Thine Own Way Lord!

It Is Not Just About Me!

"... and He died for all, that those who live should live no longer for themselves, but for Him who died for them and rose again." (2 Corinthians 5:15)

One of the greatest philosophies to adopt as a new believer, as a restored believer, or as a hungry servant of the Lord, is to never lose the sense that we are God's, and that we don't belong to anyone else!

The gospel of the kingdom of God is not just about me, it's about the expansion of His glory to all people of the earth.

In the age that we live, we must have a strong

sense of belonging to the Lord— that we were bought with a price, and we will not sell out to anyone or anything. Our commitment to Jesus must be the center of everything we think, say, and do!

Another philosophy to embrace is to always walk consciously in the will of God. Be ready to follow the Lord wherever He takes you. By this I mean that we follow without reserves, without regrets, and without retreats!

Don't be looking for the will of God— you are the will of God! Wherever the Spirit of God leads you, that is where God needs you to be. Whatever happens in your life whether good or bad, just know that the Lord has allowed that in your life for molding and shaping of your own character.

What About My Enemies?

"You have heard that it was said, 'You shall love

Chapter 11: Have Thine Own Way Lord!

your neighbor and hate your enemy.' But I say to you, love your enemies, bless those who curse you, do good to those who hate you, and pray for those who spitefully use you and persecute you, that you may be sons of your Father in heaven." (Matthew 5:43-45)

What about those wicked enemies? Those enemies are moved by the hand of God against us to make us better servants for His glory! The Lord may be stretching our faith, our compassion, our mercy, our forgiveness, or our love by sending unfair or unjust adversity our way!

We can make the attempt of rebuking them in Jesus' name, but wouldn't it be wiser to find out if the Lord is the one behind the adversity or not? Too many times we find ourselves warring against the Spirit of God thinking it's some demonic entity. We must be wiser in our walk with God!

Chapter 11: Have Thine Own Way Lord!

The Ministry of Brokenness

The ministry of brokenness has its philosophy in that we as God's servants allow the Lord to be first in everything. This lifestyle embodies the thought that we follow Christ no matter where He goes! Our call is to follow Him, no matter how inconvenient it might be to us!

It almost sounds rebellious in a way, but the Spirit of God would never lead us where God has not prepared provisions for us! As the Lord leads us by His Spirit, confirmation of His leadership will be made clear. It is not a rule of order, it is a peaceful transition of God's divine advancement.

When God is leading the way, those who are over us in spiritual authority will be able to bear witness of any transition in our lives. Make sure you get under good, solid, and biblically balanced godly leadership to guide you if and when needed!

Chapter 11: Have Thine Own Way Lord!

Should I Stay Or Should I Go?

In our walk with God, there will be many challenges. Some of these challenges will be so hard to overcome, that at times, it might seem more beneficial to quit altogether! Have you had any of these lately?

I have had many battles in my walk with God, as a servant of God, as a minister of the gospel, as a leader in His church. Too many times, people have attacked, maligned, criticized, even hated me and the work I do for some reason, and I am not sure why! Though my spirit, soul, and body have taken a toll, I will not turn back.

My Mind Has Been Made Up!

Years ago, when I gave my life to Jesus, the church I attended used to play an old chorus praise song— I Have Decided to Follow Jesus was the title. You might have heard it. When I

Chapter 11: Have Thine Own Way Lord!

would sing this song, I meant it! Here is a few stanzas to it:

I have decided to follow Jesus,
I have decided to follow Jesus,
No turning back, no turning back!

Though none go with me, still I will follow,
Though none go with me, still I will follow,
No turning back, no turning back!

Serving Jesus is a one-way ticket! Anyone who decides to follow Jesus, let him count the cost first— it might be that you don't have it in you to follow through. Walking with Jesus is definitely not for wimps!

When Jesus left heaven to come to us here on earth, he counted the cost. He knew it would cost Him everything to get the job done!

In the book of Isaiah 50:7, the Scripture says, "For

Chapter 11: Have Thine Own Way Lord!

the Lord GOD will help Me; Therefore I will not be disgraced; Therefore I have set My face like a flint, And I know that I will not be ashamed."

Who was Isaiah making reference to? He was making reference to the Messiah. Over eight-hundred years before Christ came to earth, the Prophet Isaiah saw this in the Spirit; he heard one of Christ's heart yearnings, as He knew He would be facing opposition.

Setting Your Face Like a Flint!

What does it mean to set your face like a flint anyways? Setting your face like a flint implies that you're expecting some opposition, to stand strong in the face of adversity. To set your face like a flint means to regard these difficulties as worthwhile when you consider what they will lead you to.

Unless we in our own heart have fully surren-

Chapter 11: Have Thine Own Way Lord!

dered to Jesus, (and by this, I mean to the level of martyrdom, one will always struggle to please God) please , do yourself a huge favor and count the cost. Don't embarrass yourself!

As I close this chapter, I am reminded of another hymn that revolutionized my idea of what it means to serve the Living God.

As a servant of Christ, one must not only allow God to lead, but must also embrace the road He chooses for us.

In the hymn written in the early 1900's entitled, Have Thine Own Way, the writer expresses such a burning passion to please God in all things. To be like clay in the Potter's hands is the ultimate cry. Listen to some of the lyrics:

Have Thine own way, Lord! Have Thine own way!
Thou art the Potter, I am the clay.
Mold me and make me after Thy will;

Chapter 11: Have Thine Own Way Lord!

While I am waiting, yielded and still.

Have Thine own way, Lord! Have Thine own way!
Search me and try me, Master, today!
Whiter than snow, Lord, wash me just now,
As in Thy presence humbly I bow.

"But the pot he was shaping from the clay was marred in his hands; so the potter formed it into another pot, shaping it as seemed best to him. Then the word of the Lord came to me. He said, 'Can I not do with you, Israel, as this potter does?' declares the Lord. 'Like clay in the hand of the potter, so are you in my hand, Israel.'" (Jeremiah 18:4-6)

As you pursue God, always keep this philosophy before you: He is the Potter; We are the clay. This is divine order!

Chapter 12

In Case of Floods!

"When the enemy comes in like a flood,
The Spirit of the Lord will lift up a standard against him." (Isaiah 59:19b)

I have taken some time to share some of the most powerful principles for obtaining victory in the life of the servant of God. All the chapters of this manuscript have been written out of pure passion to pursue the heart of God— the zeal to go deeper into His purposes and find true joy while doing it.

As I near the closing of this book, I would like to add this final chapter about floods— spiritual floods. I have read hundreds of books in my lifetime, and I have yet to read a book that gave a chapter about overcoming discouragement, oppression, fear, anxiety, guilt, and shame and the

Chapter 12: In Case of Floods!

awkward emotions of feeling lost, confused and in chaos! Do you know what I mean?

Who said that Christians don't go through turmoil? Who are those who say that being a Christian is a simple walk in the park? Where are the false prophets who say, Just confess it and it will all go away?

It's Only a Fiery Trial!

Before I get a little deeper into our chapter, let me just say that not all servants of the Lord go through spiritual floods; some just go through the fiery trial, a fiery dart of the enemy and nothing more.

Usually, the fiery darts are for those who are in an infantile state with Jesus— they are experiencing the basic trials of life that come our way as we learn to obey Christ. The Apostle Peter said this regarding these trials: "Beloved, do not think it strange concerning the fiery trial which is to try you, as though some strange thing happened to you." (1 Peter 4:12)

Fiery trials are adversities and afflictions that we go through daily. Nothing really hard but maybe a bit challenging still. We can usually pray and overcome them by making our faith and confidence sure. The night may get dark, but we have the assurance that it will pass, and the morning will come soon. Normally, we all prevail when faced with fiery trials.

What About Spiritual Floods?

What is a spiritual flood? What is the magnitude of such a trial? Floods are intense methods used by God to break a man or a woman down. It is used to bring one to the realization that they are nothing but dust, and unless one realizes this, the flood will never subside.

Chapter 12: In Case of Floods!

The facts are the facts: God oversees our lives, but may allow the devil to have his way with us at times. Remember, the devil is on a leash. He will not be allowed to go any further than what God wants!

An interesting portion of God's word says, "God will raise up a standard against him (the enemy)."

In other words, when the enemy comes in like a flood, (not a fiery dart) the Spirit of the Lord will lift a standard against him. What does this mean?

What this means is that when you are being flooded by the enemy, God will by His force, take the enemy out of your life. He will step into your situation and carry you on eagle's wings!

You and I have been through different and varying trials. Some have been very challenging and others extremely challenging. They have come in waves and sometimes even as multiples. Yet, in all these things, the Lord has sustained us. You are a better servant of God because of it!

What Does a Flood Look Like?

Discouragement. I believe that everyone has dealt with discouragement in their life. Some of it has been easily overcome, but there is another kind that holds on to us until our spiritual life is paralyzed. I met a man who went through severe discouragement a few years ago— the man couldn't not shake it off until it paralyzed him. He was a servant of the Lord and had a very powerful ministry. He knew it, but the devil also knew it. The devil attacked him over and over; the enemy flooded his mind with despair, and he gave everything up! I believe this man met his hour of testing —his own spiritual flood. In the early years of my own ministry, I too faced a spiritual flood. It was so severe that it almost

Chapter 12: In Case of Floods!

cost my ministry. A couple who vowed to be faithful to our ministry were my associates and they were very helpful initially, until they decided that people followed them more than they did me as their pastor. The people followed them out of our church and fractured the work we had worked so hard for. As a young pastor, I was devastated. I didn't want to continue anymore and decided to quit the ministry. No sooner had I made up my mind when the audible voice of God came to me. The Lord said to me, David, you will dream again. This is not over. I will establish you. Just don't give up!

It was the voice of God that saved me from quitting! He will do the same for you, just wait upon the Lord, and again, I say wait!

Oppressed by the Devil. When we commit a transgression against the Lord, the first one to point it out is the devil himself. He will call you out for any wrongdoing! I believe that if one

Chapter 12: In Case of Floods!

walks in unforgiveness, in rebellion against authority, in total disobedience to the known will of God, one will always feel oppressed by the enemy! He takes advantage of our weaknesses and makes every effort to keep us down by putting his foot on our necks. The devil is a good devil at what he does. He knows that believers constantly fall into guilt and condemnation, so he takes advantage of this. The feeling of never being able to measure up to God's rules is something the devil torments God's children with. He brings about the idea that we are just miserable human beings who never got it together! Though this may be true, and though his calling out is also true and we stand guilty of all charges, yet God is still able to make us stand and present us holy and blameless at the return of Christ. When we feel that we are constantly being flooded with thoughts of defeat and the never-ending introspection of our souls, my friend, we are being oppressed by the enemy. My advice is: Get washed in the blood, confess

Chapter 12: In Case of Floods!

all your sins to God, and enter His forgiveness by faith. The devil must then flee!

Fear. Have you ever been afraid? I am sure that you have been. We all have been afraid. Yet there is a fear that also paralyzes our forward motion. Fear is truly a demonic trap to keep you and I from advancing into God's purpose. I heard a man once say that the last 15 seconds of fear were the hardest! Faith is the opposite of fear. The Scripture says that perfect love casts away all fear. If we believe God and have the faith to believe that God will keep us, then we will advance. If we don't have faith, then fear will set in and paralyze our forward motion. Too many of us have been paralyzed by fear in countless areas for too many years. We can overcome simple trials, but there are those trials that we hate to face simply because we can't overcome them. It is time to rise in the faith of God and cross over the Jordan River into our Promised Land!

Chapter 12: In Case of Floods!

Guilt & Shame. Guilt and shame are emotions that make us feel like losers! Have you felt like a loser lately? Maybe a transgression has been committed and you feel extreme guilt. The enemy will try to remind you that you have not been forgiven by the blood of Jesus, and that you are still guilty of what you have done. Have you experienced this? I have. Let me tell you: There is a type of guilt and shame that hangs on to us when we have transgressed against one or more of God's laws. Guilt and shame are signs to our conscience that we have wronged God and others. Worse yet, there is a certain guilt and shame that won't leave us alone; it digs deep into our spirit and makes us doubt God's forgiveness. At this point, we have entered doubt and feel the rejection of God. Although we have not been rejected, the devil tells us we have. The devil usually will step in and say to us, You are not forgiven, you are still in your sins, God will punish you for it! My friends, let me just say that guilt and shame will cling to us until we get under the redeeming power of the blood of Jesus. Once we are covered by His precious blood, guilt and shame must go. If it doesn't go immediately, it will eventually. Hang on to the act of faith you did when you asked for forgiveness, the emotion will come later.

Nights of Confusion. In nights of confusion, the struggle has to do with not knowing what is happening in you and around you. As a matter of fact, this method being used to test our character, must be one of the hardest of all tests! I do believe that God will allow us to go through different tests, but for those who want to be servants of God, they will have to face the flood with nights of confusion. What does this really look like? Well for starters, Job was trying to get a handle on all that was happening to him. He looked for rest in the Lord— but couldn't even find Him! How about that for a real test? The One who made you and knows you better than any human being, is not even present! Have you had nights where you feel all alone? Nights where those who love you the most, don't even have an answer for you? You make the effort in trying to change the situation, but all you get is nothing but silence— dead silence. This is what I am talking about. If you have been through some of this, then you are facing the flood! What do you do when facing nights of confusion? You learn to ride out the storm. Ride it out by staying; don't try or do anything crazy. Allow the night to teach you to wait upon His faithfulness. The Scripture says that ". . . weeping may endure for a night, but joy comes in the morning." [see Psalm 30:5b] Hang on to the hem of His garment! [see Matthew 9:20-21] Your deliverance is coming speedily! [see Luke 18:1-8]

Many More Floods . . .

The list I presented to you in this final chapter for what I believe are floods, are not the only floods that come our way. There are many more.

Chapter 12: In Case of Floods!

Remember, all these floods that come our way are meant to squeeze the honey out of us. They are not given so they can kill us, though it may seem that way. But they are given for another type of killing— the killing of self! Remember the words of John the Baptist, "He must increase, I must decrease." [see John 3:30]

My Final Thought: God Is Able to Make Us Stand!

Let me just say as I finish my manuscript, it doesn't matter what you are facing in your life today, I tell you, God is able to make you stand! There is no storm so strong that Jesus can't quench; there is no failure that God can't turn around; there is no sin so wicked that God can't forgive; there is no emotional distress so deep, that God can't transform by His mighty power!

I have served King Jesus for over thirty-five years, and I have yet to experience failure coming from

Chapter 12: In Case of Floods!

Him! He is faithful and will remain faithful to the end!

If you fall, be quick to get back up! It is never how many times you fall, but how quickly you get up and continue your journey. Stay faithful in your journey no matter how long, dry, challenging, lonely, inconvenient, isolated, and heart-wrenching it might be. If you are experiencing any of these things I just mentioned, just wait upon the Lord till His mercy comes. Listen to what the great Psalmist left us:

> "Unto You I lift up my eyes,
> O You who dwell in the heavens.
> Behold, as the eyes of servants look to the hand of their masters,
> As the eyes of a maid to the hand of her mistress,
> So our eyes look to the Lord our God,
> Until He has mercy on us."
> (Psalm 123:1, 2)

For the Purchase of More Books
by David Mayorga

Visit our Online Bookstore at

www.shabarpublications.com

www.ingramcontent.com/pod-product-compliance
Lightning Source LLC
Chambersburg PA
CBHW071454070526
44578CB00001B/341